ISBN 978-0-331-70387-0
PIBN 10828503

Technical and Bibliographic Notes / Notes techniques et bibliographiques

e has attempted to obtain the best original
le for filming. Features of this copy which
ographically unique, which may alter any
s in the reproduction, or which may
change the usual method of filming, are
ow.

L'Institut a microfilmé le meilleur exempla
lui a été possible de se procurer. Les détail
exemplaire qui sont peut-être uniques du p
bibliographique, qui peuvent modifier une
reproduite, ou qui peuvent exiger une moc
dans la méthode normale de filmage sont i
ci-dessous.

red covers/
rture de couleur

□ Coloured pages/
Pages de couleur

damaged/
rture endommagée

☑ Pages damaged/
Pages endommagées

restored and/or laminated/
rture restaurée et/ou pelliculée

□ Pages restored and/or laminated/
Pages restaurées et/ou pelliculées

title missing/
re de couverture manque

☑ Pages discoloured, stained or foxed/
Pages décolorées, tachetées ou piquée

red maps/
géographiques en couleur

□ Pages detached/
Pages détachées

red ink (i.e. other than blue or black)/
de couleur (i.e. autre que bleue ou noire)

☑ Showthrough/
Transparence

red plates and/or illustrations/
hes et/ou illustrations en couleur

□ Quality of print varies/
Qualité inégale de l'impression

d with other material/
avec d'autres documents

□ Continuous pagination/
Pagination continue

binding may cause shadows or distortion
interior margin/
ure serrée peut causer de l'ombre ou de la
sion le long de la marge intérieure

□ Includes index(es)/
Comprend un (des) index

Title on header taken from /
Le titre de l'en-tête provient·

leaves added during restoration may appear
n the text. Whenever possible, these have
omitted from filming/
eut que certaines pages blanches ajoutées
'une restauration apparaissent dans le texte,
lorsque cela etait possible, ces pages n'ont
é filmées.

□ Title page of issue/
Page de titre de la livraison

□ Caption of issue/
Titre de départ de la livraison

□ Masthead/
Générique (périodiques) de la livraiso

The copy filmed here has been reproduced thanks to the generosity of:

Archives of Ontario
Toronto

The images appearing here are the best quality possible considering the condition and legibility of the original copy and in keeping with the filming contract specifications.

Original copies in printed paper covers are filmed beginning with the front cover and ending on the last page with a printed or illustrated impression, or the back cover when appropriate. All other original copies are filmed beginning on the first page with a printed or illustrated impression, and ending on the last page with a printed or illustrated impression.

The last recorded frame on each microfiche shall contain the symbol ➔ (meaning "CONTINUED"), or the symbol ▽ (meaning "END"), whichever applies.

Maps, plates, charts, etc., may be filmed at different reduction ratios. Those too large to be entirely included in one exposure are filmed beginning in the upper left hand corner, left to right and top to bottom, as many frames as required. The following diagrams illustrate the method:

1   **2**   **3**

3

1

2

3

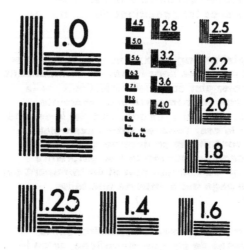

MICROCOPY RESOLUTION TEST CHART
NATIONAL BUREAU OF STANDARDS
STANDARD REFERENCE MATERIAL 1010a
(ANSI and ISO TEST CHART No 2)

James Hogg

The
Ettrick Shepherd

By

Professor John Ferguson, M.A., M.D.,
Toronto University

TORONTO

1913

James Hogg

The
Ettrick Shepherd

By

Professor John Ferguson, M.A., M.D.,
Toronto University

TORONTO

1913

JAMES HOGG

THE ETTRICK SHEPHERD

THE exact date of Hogg's birth is not known, but the register of his native parish contains the entry that he was baptized on the ninth of December, 1770. It is definitely known that he passed into that world of which he sang and wrote so much on the 21st of November, 1835. He thus lived most likely to see his sixty-fifth birthday. These were wonderful years in the history of Britain, and especially in that of Scotland. In addition to covering the life of Hogg, they included the last twenty-six years of Robert Burns', and all of Sir Walter Scott's life. There is only one other country which produced three great poets in such a short period under conditions so peculiar, and that country was Greece, in her golden age, when she gave to the world Aeschylus, Sophocles, and Euripides. Let us look into the life and writings of Hogg, and try to ascertain wherein they should claim our attention, and to what extent Hogg made Scotland and the world of letters his debtor, for surely the legacy he bequeathed is both large and of most precious material. In the words of Milton:—

> "He, above the rest
> In shape and gesture proudly eminent,
> Stood like a tower."

I do not place Hogg above Scott and Burns, but I place him with them, and these three are among the very greatest of Scotland's gifts to mankind. All three were true sons of the people, and all were true sons of genius. Scotland cannot afford to forget her literary trinity, in order of their birth, Burns, Hogg, Scott.

It has been said that his life was uneventful. No life of a genius is ever such. We know but little of the real life of Homer, but what would not the world have lost without the Iliad! The quiet life of Virgil sinks into nothing as compared with his immortal epic, the Aeneid! The many years that Gray spent in meditation over the tombs gave us the Elegy! All sane men would rather be Milton with his Paradise Lost in his hand, than Napoleon with his many victories at the cost of rivers of human blood! So, too, of Hogg. The long summer days he spent on the hillside, under the sky's blue dome, which gave birth to Kilmeny and his songs, is a far greater event than the stirring days of Queen Mary, or the murderous career of Claverhouse. Hogg had a message for his fellowmen, it was a great message, and that message remains with us. The birth of Shakespeare was a far more noted event than that of James the Sixth of Scotland, and first of England. Thus it is that the appearance of the prophet, the teacher, the poet, is ever a great event; and so the coming of Hogg among his people must be regarded.

> "He made his prophets poets, and the more
> We feel of poesy, do we become
> Like God in love and power."

Had Bailey lived in Hogg's day, he could not have uttered words that could have better befitted that pure and noble poetic soul.

Hogg's life was a strenuous one. He had a hard struggle for the bare necessities of life, he had a hard struggle, indeed for what education he acquired, and he had a hard struggle to gain recognition at the hands of the publisher and the people. They had a great man in their midst and for long they knew it not. But as Elijah could commune with nature and nature's God while hiding by the lonely brook, so could Hogg find inspiration as he says himself in "rocks that seemed to prop the skies." About his eighth and ninth years, for a few months each winter, he attended school, and from that onward he received no formal education. But he had his schools and schoolmasters of a far other kind, as had another great Scotchman, in the person of Hugh Miller. His mother, Margaret Laidlaw, was deeply versed in Scotch tradition, legend, tune, and song. From her he learned much that bore splendid fruit later on in his writings. He could truly say with the great Goethe, "I got my stature from my father, and my inner man from my mother."

But Hogg had other teachers. He was in close touch with nature in her wildest and most poetic forms. The wild storm and the dark and gloomy winter's day; the rushing torrent brimful, hastening down the mountain side and through the glen, on its mad course to the sea; the lofty and rugged hills that tossed their heads far up into the blue dome above; the forests and the meadows, opening their richest hues to the life-giving beams of spring's returning sun, and the peaceful flocks grazing over the lea, all raised his thoughts from nature to the supernatural. These influences would cause a spirit like his to expand as does the blossom to the vernal rays.

Lacking in education, in books, in learned companions, and unable to write, he had a hard struggle to find an outlet for his aspiring soul. He was twenty-five before he learned to write, and then by careful copying such bits of script as might come his way. He practised the making of the letters on flat stones while herding his flocks, yet he at last acquired an easy and dignified style of penmanship, and his manuscripts contained almost no errors in spelling or faults in syntax. All this brings to one's mind the words which Shakespeare makes Cæsar say:—

"Nor stony towers, nor walls of beaten brass,
Nor airless dungeons, nor strong links of iron
Can be retentive of the strength of spirit."

So Hogg, despite the many hardships of youth and early manhood, and the chill penury that might have frozen the genial current of his soul, burst through all barriers and became one of Scotland's greatest sons, and one of the few and immortal names that are not born to die.

Hogg was sprung from a long line of shepherd peasants. They lived in a poor district where there was a very meagre supply of the world's goods. The country was romantic and rich in the finest scenery. It was also full of splendid legend and the story of brave deeds. Every foot of the Ettrick and the Yarrow could tell of some noble person who had died for the sake of freedom of country or liberty of conscience. Some of his ancestors are said to have had associations with those of the spirit world, as tradition in those days ran. While he may not have believed all this, it no doubt helped to make him what he was, namely, the poet of the mystic feelings and the supernatural.

In appearance he was of handsome form. Those who knew him describe him in his early manhood as of medium height, finely symmetrical and agile in form, of a clear, ruddy face full of the emotion of hope, with a profusion of light brown hair that fell over his shoulders, and beaming light blue eyes that gave expression to the pure and gifted mind within. The famous painting of him by Sir John Watson Gordon, taken when he was about fifty-five, shows him seated, with his broad plaid passing across his breast and over his left shoulder, then loosely resting on his left arm. His left hand is reposing on the curved end of his great stick that was his life-long companion. The collar of his coat rolls well away from his neck and out towards his shoulders. His face is full and of oval form and clean-shaven, with the exception of a portion of the beard left on either side in front of and below the ears. There is an abundance of wavy, curly hair, now turning gray, rising over his arched forehead. The contour of the nose, the eyebrows, and the lines of the mouth give one to feel that the painting is that of no ordinary man. It is truly the work of a great artist on a still greater subject. To such a face we can fittingly apply the words of Sir Walter Scott:—

"There was a soft and pensive grace,
  A cast of thought upon the face
  That suited well the forehead high,
  The eyelash dark, and downcast eye;
  The mild expression spoke a mind
  In duty firm, composed, resigned."

Let us now review a few of the incidents in Hogg's life. His father, Robert, was a small farmer, and lost everything through bad times, and the absconding of one of his debtors. He had to return to his original calling of shepherd. This rendered it impossible to give any more than the most meagre education. James was hired out as a herd lad while only six years of age. His genial and kindly nature made him a favorite with his employers.

While quite young he was hired by a Mr. Laidlaw. When in his 16th year, or in 1786, he engaged with a second Mr. Laidlaw, with whom he remained for three years. Mrs. Laidlaw was very kind to him and gave him some books to read, among which may be mentioned Blind Harry's Life and Adventures of Wallace, Ramsay's Gentle Shepherd, and Burnett's Theory of the Conflagration of the Earth. Hogg says himself that if he had not read this last on the hillside in the bright sunlight, it would have deranged his reason. When he was nineteen years of age, or in 1789, he entered the service of a third Mr. Laidlaw, of Blackhouse, in Yarrow. Here he received much consideration. Mr. Laidlaw had many books and these were freely put at the disposal of Hogg. It was here that he acquired his fondness for reading, and when about 25 years of age began to learn to write. It was at this time that he made the acquaintance of another William Laidlaw, who became Sir Walter Scott's amanuensis, and who stood at the death-bed of both Scott and Hogg.

It was during September of 1796, about two months after the death of Burns, that a remarkable incident occurred. Hogg was on the green hillside watching the flocks of his master, when he was joined by a sort of daft character, named Jack Scott. He began reciting Burns' Tam O'Shanter. At this time Hogg had not heard of Burns. He was so much impressed with the poem that he made Jack Scott repeat it until he had learned it. He then resolved to follow in the footsteps of the Ayrshire poet, an ambition which never left him.

In 1800, Hogg made a visit to Edinburgh on business for Mr. Laidlaw. It was on this occasion that he sang Donald McDonald. He was asked to publish it, which he did anonymously. It became very popular, but did not bring fame to the author, as the public did not know who was the author. On his return from Edinburgh, Mr. Laidlaw introduced Sir Walter Scott to Hogg, and a fast friendship was thus established, that was only once interrupted for a short period through a misunderstanding on the part of the latter. Scott was greatly pleased with Hogg's mother, and took down from her recitation many of the old ballads referring to the deeds of the Scots and Laidlaws. It was at this period, also, that his brother William married, whereupon he took another farm. This made it necessary for James to leave the service of Mr. Laidlaw and take up the management of Ettrick House, as his parents were now becoming advanced in years. This did not pay, and at the end of the lease he gave up the farm. He forsaw that the farming of Ettrick House would not pay, and this induced him to make a tour of the Highlands in search of employment. He was unsuccessful. It was not long after this when he made a second trip to the west of the Highlands. It was on this occasion that he decided to lease a farm on the Island of Harris, one of the Hebrides. He invested £200 on this venture, but found that the title was in dispute and he lost all he had advanced. He was involved in debt and had to flee to Cumberland for some time, but in a year returned and engaged with a farmer in Nithsdale.

This gave rise to a crisis in Hogg's life, and he determined to visit Sir Walter Scott and seek his advice. Scott urged him to make a collection of some of his poems and publish them, and with this end in view introduced Hogg to Constable. That publisher agreed to bring out a volume of Hogg's poems if two hundred subscribers were guaranteed. The author soon had five hundred names on his list and the volume, known as the Mountain Bard, made its appearance. This venture realized for the author £300.

No sooner was Hogg in possession of the funds than he took a farm at Carfarden, in Dumfriesshire. He was soon involved in an expensive lawsuit with his landlord, ending in the loss of everything, as had been his bitter experiences with the farm in the Hebrides. While at Carfarden he made the acquaintance of Mr. Macturk of Stenhouse. Hogg prized this friendship so much that he said it fully made up for his losses. This is in keeping with his character and reveals one phase of the real man, that a true friendship is worth more than money, and is cheap at any price. To Mr. Macturk he wrote: "Perhaps the very circumstance of being initiated into the mysteries of your character is of itself sufficient compensation for all I suffered in your country."

During the next few years we do not hear much of Hogg. About the only thing he did was to issue a volume called the Forest Minstrel. This brought to him a donation from the Duchess of Buccleuch of £100. This brings us to 1810 when we find Hogg in Edinburgh engaged in the publication of the *Spy*. This periodical ran for about a year. The enterprise made for him some enemies, no money, considerable reputation, and a few loyal friends, among whom may be mentioned James Gray, of the High School, John Sym, or Timothy Tickler, of the *Notes*, Thomas

Gillespie, a professor in St. Andrews, Rev. William Gillespie, of Kells, J Black, of the *Morning Chronicle*, and Grieve and his partner, Scott, who carried on a tailoring establishment in Edinburgh. Following the failure of the *Spy*, the shepherd poet, along with a few others, started a school of oratory, or sort of debating club, conducted on parliamentary lines, and to which the public was admitted for a small fee. As may be presumed this put no money in the pockets of the promoters, and Hogg was reduced to the condition of absolute want, and was supported for about six months by his right loyal friends Grieve and Scott, the tailors. The assistance of these was like the shower to the thirsty blossom, and so we can say of it in the words of Robert Browning:—

"What joy is better than the news of friends
Whose memories were a solace to me oft,
As mountain baths to wild fowls in their flight."

But out of one of these dark days came one of Hogg's greatest gifts to literature. With the assistance of Grieve, our poet gathered up some of the pieces that had appeared in the *Spy* and linked them properly together, with additions, and produced "The Queen's Wake." This was in 1813, when the author was in his 43rd year.

Strange longings came over Hogg at this period to return to his loved Ettrick and Yarrow and enjoy his communion with nature among the hills and in the glens, and to wander once more along the romantic banks of the river. With these feelings rising in his heart he wrote the Duchess of Buccleuch in these words: "There is a certain poor bard, who has two old parents, each of them upwards of eighty years of age, and that bard has no house nor home to shelter these poor parents in, or cheer the evening of their lives. A single line from a certain very great and very beautiful lady, to a certain Mr. Riddell, would insure that small pendicle to the bard at once. But she will grant no such thing! I appeal to your grace if she is not a very bad lady that!" The poet's request was not immediately answered. Five months later, when the Duchess died, she made her husband promise that he would not forget her poor bard. As a result of this request the Duke gave him for life rent-free the farm at Altrive. Towards this lovely spot the shepherd set his face.

But money was required to stock the farm, and our poet had none; and, more, he had drawn to the limit upon the generosity of his friends. He now bethought himself a rather remarkable experiment in the literary world. He wrote to such poets as Wordsworth, Coleridge, Byron, Southey, Rogers, Pringle, and others, asking them for an original poem to make up a volume to be called the "Poetic Mirror." Sir Walter Scott at once refused with the statement that "every herring must hing on its ane head." This caused the rupture in the friendship between Hogg and Scott that has been mentioned and which lasted for some months. Most of the others promised but did not fulfil their undertaking. In the meantime Hogg had entered into an arrangement to have the volume brought out. When the promised poems were not forthcoming, our poet set himself to work to write original poems in imitation of the style of the respective auth who had promised a contribution. All this he did in three months, and the work was so well done that it passed off for several months undetected. When the real nature of these poems became known, Hogg joined most heartily in the laugh. This was a wonderful achievement for it was no easy task to choose so many topics and reproduce the styles of such widely different writers as Byron, Wordsworth, Coleridge, etc. On a former occasion DeQuincey and Hogg were dining with Wordsworth at Ryedale Mount, the home of the latter. On that evening there was a beautiful aurora borealis, and Miss Wordsworth said she hoped it was not a precursor of some evil. Hogg replied by saying, "Hoot, mam, it is only a triumphal arch in honor o' the meeting o' the poets." At this remark Wordsworth whispered to DeQuincey, "Poets! Poets! What does the fellow mean? Where are the poets?" When DeQuincey afterwards told this to Hogg, he became very indignant at Wordsworth; and this afforded the excuse for the terrible travesty of Wordsworth's style which Hogg introduced into his "Poetic Mirror."

About 1815, when Hogg was 45, he was very busy on his literary work; and partly from new productions and partly from new editions of former works, he amassed about £1,000. It was at this time that along with Thomas Pringle, he took an active part in starting Blackwood's Magazine. In 1820 he married Margaret Phillips, who was to receive from her father £1,000. Hogg now took a nine years' lease of Mount Benger. This proved a most disastrous venture. His father-in-law failed and could not pay the amount due his daughter. There was thus a shortage of money and all that went into the farm was lost. He made a brave effort to hold his ground by writing stories. When freed from this lease he again retired to Altrive Lake to the farm granted him for life by the Duke of Buccleuch.

The closing years of his life were sad enough.

In 1831 he visited London with the object of arranging for the publication of a complete edition of his writings. This he did with Cochrane, the publisher. On 25th January, 1832, he was banqueted in London, with Sir John Malcolm in the chair, and two sons of Robert Burns seated by his side. He left London with his heart full of hope; but he was scarcely arrived home when he received word that Cochrane had failed and only one volume issued. His hopes were again dashed to the ground.

After his return from London he was tendered a banquet in Peebles. On this occasion Professor John Wilson, known as Christopher North, occupied the chair. It was then that Hogg said: "I have sought fame while yet among the mountains I carried the crook and the plaid. I had sought it in the city; and now when I see so many talented men around me, and met on my account, well might I exclaim, 'I have found it at last.'"

In 1834, Cochrane had started in business again, and undertook to issue a complete edition of Hogg's writings. This time he sent forth three volumes, when he again failed. This last misfortune weighed heavily upon him and his health began to give way. After three or four weeks of severe suffering his brave and pure soul passed away to join that spirit world of which he had thought and written so much. He died as peacefully as if taking a sleep on the side of a moorland rill wrapped in his grey plaid. He was buried in Ettrick churchyard, close to the church in which he was baptized, and a few yards from the cottage in which he was born. His widow raised a simple stone to his memory, bearing his name, the date of his birth and death, and a minstrel harp; and she planted the sod with daisies brought from the Yarrow. Over his ashes we can recall the words of Shakespeare in his "Two Gentlemen of Verona":—

> "His words were bonds, his oaths were oracles,
> His love sincere, his thoughts immaculate,
> His tears pure messengers sent from his heart,
> His heart as far from fraud as heaven from earth."

For his opportunities Hogg wrote much. He was not like Wordsworth or Carlyle, or Dickens, or Scott, or Ruskin, one who devoted his whole time and energy to his literary pursuits. He was twenty-five before he could write, and nearly twenty before he had access to any other books than the Bible, the Scottish version of the Psalms, and two or three old books. Like Burns, what he has left us is a mere fragment of what was possible; but for that fragment we are profoundly thankful. His life was a hard one; indeed, many and severe were his disappointments. In his own words:

> " 'Tis ↄ ↄe we hae had mony sorrows and crosses,
> Our pouches oft toom, and our hearts fu' o' care."

But he labored on bravely to the last, in the fullest confidence that the future would preserve what the past had inspired.

His prose writings have unique historical value. He did not invent his material. He took the traditions of the people, the crude anecdotes as he found them, and by careful investigation tested their accuracy, and then clothed the whole in his own simple but charming style. These stories, therefore, are the truest kind of history; for they tell us verily what the people did, what they believed, and what they said. In these stories we learn what would be otherwise forever lost; and what a loss that would be! What would we know of the ancient Greeks without the Agamemnon, the Antigone and the Alcestes?

The simple religious faith of the Scottish people, their belief in the supernatural, the depth of their love, their intense patriotism, their unflinching heroism, their contentment with their hard lot, their trust in Divine providence, are all reflected in these tales of the Ettrick Shepherd as in a perfect mirror. I would rather study history in such writings than in those of Hallam, May or Stubbs. They give us history in the making.

Throughout his novels, tales, historical romances, the lay sermons, the life of Sir Walter Scott, and other prose writings, the language is simple, clear, and energetic. The periods are smooth with so much real verve that they afford genuine pleasure to the reader. If these writings have not the broad, even flow found in those from the pen of Scott, or that fine richness of style peculiar to Ruskin, they are never carelessly done nor lacking in freedom of phraseology. He adopts the narrative form mainly, and frequently makes his characters converse as is usual in the novel and the drama. Indeed, many of his stories are real prose tragedies. There was, at times, a fine vein of fun and always one of true humor in him. His philosophy of life was that wrong reaped its due punishment, that virtue carried with it its own reward, and that the only anchor of life was faith in the Supreme Being. In this way it is that everything became so intensely realistic to his mind. Nothing is in vain, and all is of God, whether in the natural or the spiritual world. His ghosts are as true participants in the affairs of men as was that of Hamlet's father, and his witches play the same essential *role* as did the three that met Macbeth on the blasted heath. Hogg, like Shakespeare, might not have believed that such apparitions did actually exist; but, like Shakespeare, he was dealing with the beliefs and traditions of the people, and followed the words of Othello, "Nothing extenuate, nor set down aught in malice."

It would be impossible to give specimens of Hogg's prose, as his style is so varied. A few selections would convey the most meagre conception of what he really did, so that one must have recourse to his many tales to form anything like an adequate idea of the wide range of his mind, his sympathies, and his descriptive powers. For every sorrow he had a tear, for every joy a smile, and for every needy one a helping hand. In his moods he can change with the demands of his theme. He can be as plaintive as the wail of a child, as we find revealed in the story of "Mary Montgomery;" or as pathetic ı the sobs of the widow as we find her weeping over the body of her murdered husband in the tale of "John Weir;" or he can stir the feelings and emotions to their very depths and make the very blood run cold as in that record of human cruelty and revenge, where, in "Adam Bell," the heart is shown at its sternest and worst; or he can take us by the hand into the very precincts of the mystery of the spirit world and fill us with awe as we feel that the spirits of the two mysterious white hounds were those of Ellen and . ꞌ . of Rosaline, as we learn in the legend ꞌ ue "Eildon Hunt." To do this is not the work of an ordinary mind; but rather the achievement of one whose imagination was constructed after the fashion of a Shelley, or, indeed, as was that of the immortal bard of Stratford-on-Avon. This phase of the Ettrick Shepherd's mind has not received the attention which it merits: Like Shakespeare he saw men and women as they were, and with the eye of the soul, as Shakespeare tells us, he saw much of the spirit world that animates all:—

17

> "The poet's eye in a fine frenzy rolling,
> Doth glance from heaven to earth, from earth
> to heaven,
> And, as imagination bodies forth
> The forms of things unknown, the poet's pen
> Twines them to shapes, and gives to airy
> nothing
> A local habitation and a name."

This is true of Hogg's prose as it is of his poetry; for, in his prose, he is ever the poet; and thus it is that his stories are dramas.

We cannot pursue this subject further, though only the fringe of a proper study of his prose writings has been touched upon. It behoves us now to give some attention to his poetry; for he was a poet. Professor John Wilson tells us that "Hogg was the only worthy successor of Burns," and Professor Veitch declares that "After Burns, Hogg was the greatest poet that has sprung from the bosom of the common people." As a poet he was the author of "The Queen's Wake," "The Mountain Bard," "The Pilgrims of the Sun," "The Pedlar," "The Poetic Mirror," "Mador of the Moor" "Queen Hynde," Ballads and Poems, Songs, Sacred Pieces, and a number of miscellaneous poems. When one considers the length and quality of these poetic productions, they constitute a remarkable addition to the world's literature for which we, as Scotchmen, are justly proud.

> "He seized his country's lyre
> With ardent grasp and strong,
> And made his soul of fire
> Dissolve itself in song."

Let us view Hogg's poetry from a few of the crucial tests of all poetry—tests to which all poetry must conform, and failing in which the author cannot lay claim to what the poet should ever be, a prophet and a teacher. To those most capable of judging we appeal in full confidence.

First, his descriptive power. To paint a scene with the brush and colors is a work of art. To paint it in words is also a work of art; but it is very high art. As a painter of scenes, real and imaginary, Hogg ranks with the great seers who saw visions and dreamt dreams. Take the following from ' The Queen's Wake'':—

> "The bard on Ettrick's mountain green,
> In Nature's bosom nursed had been,
> And oft had marked, in forest lone,
> Her beauties on her mountain throne;
> Had seen her deck the wildwood tree,
> And star with snowy gems the lea;
> In loveliest colors paint the plain,
> And sow the moor with purple grain;
> By golden mead, and mountain sheer,
> Had viewed the Ettrick waving clear,
> Where shadowy flocks of purest snow
> Seemed grazing in a world below."

As one reads these lines he feels himself on the hillside, looking down upon the hawthorn hoar and the flowery meadow, through which is winding the silver stream between its mossy and verdant banks. You have, in a word, a perfect picture called up before the mind's eye, and at once we are alongside of the poet viewing that charming spot of a hundred years ago. But let us take another passage, also from "The Queen's Wake," in which the poet is describing the human form divine, in the person of Queen Mary herself.

> "Light on her airy steed she sprung,
> Around with golden tassels hung,
> No chieftain there rode half so free,
> Or half so light and gracefully.
> How sweet to see her ringlets pale
> Wild waving in the southland gale,
> Which through broom wood blossoms flew,
> To fan her cheeks of rosy hue!
> Whene'er it heaved her bosom's screen,
> What beauties in her form were seen."

There you see Queen Mary with a vividness

equal to that of having been one of the throng which welcomed her on that day home to her own country. In the following passage the beauty of the Queen is extolled, and the poet, rises to the level of Homer at his best. The scene is that of the hall in Holyrood Palace with Mary surrounded by her lords and ladies:

"There such a scene entranced the view,
   As heart of poet ever knew.
'Twas not the flush of golden gear,
Nor blaze of silver chandelier;
Nor Scotland's chiefs of noble air,
Nor dazzling rows of ladies fair;
'Twas one enthroned the rest above—
Sure 'twas the Queen of grace and love!
Taper the form, and fair the breast
Yon radiant, golden zones invest,
Where the vexed rubies blanch in death,
Beneath yon lips and balmy breath;
Coronal gems of every dye
Look dim above yon beaming eye.
Yon cheeks outvie the dawning's glow,
Red shadowed on a wreath of snow."

The following lines taken, from the "Third Night's Contest," reveal Hogg's power to handle the sublime in nature:—

"The storm had ceased to shroud the hill;
   The morning's breath was pure and chill;
And when the sun rose from the main,
No eye the glory could sustain.
The icicles so dazzling bright;
The spreading wold so smooth and white;
The cloudless sky, the air so sheen,
That roes on Pentland top were seen;
And Grampian mountain, frowning high,
Seer᾽d frozen 'mid the northern sky."

Some may claim that in these passages Hogg was inspired by the subject. He had before him the beautiful Queen Mary or the grand old scenery of Scotland. If such there be who take this view the answer is found in the Mountain Bard in what he sang of the sister of a poor man, the only thing that is known of her being that her name was Jean:—

"Her hair was like the threads o' gowd,
 Her cheeks of rosy hue,
Her e'en were like the hunting hawk's
 That ower the castle flew.

"Of fairest fashion was her form,
 Her skin the driven snow
That's drifted by the wintry storm
 On lofty Gilman's law.

"Her brow nae blink of scorning wore,
 Her teeth were ivory,
Her lips the little purple flower
 That blossoms on Bailey-lee."

Thus far we have seen Hogg's wonderful
capacity for describing scenes and persons.
He is graphic, charming and delicate. But
he had marvellous gifts for creating scenes
and persons that were pure products of his
imagination, and making them pass before the
mind's eye as splendid realities. We find
beautiful examples of this poetic power, both
to invent and portray, in "The Pilgrims of the
Sun" and in "Little Pynkie," a counterpart
to which we meet in Shakespeare alone; and
higher praise than this can come to no man.

Second, his teachings on Life. On man's
duty to man and to his country, Hogg had
clear views and expressed these in strong and
abiding form. As has been said, the poet
must be a prophet and a teacher. On the
subject of the domestic affections we find
many beautiful passages. The mother's love for
her child has been the theme of many a writer.
The following lines, which set forth a mother's
sorrow over the death of her little cherub,
would unlock any heart and find way therein:

"My sweet little cherub, how calm thou'rt reposing!
Thy suffering is over, thy mild eye is closing;
This world was to thee a step-dame unfriendly;
But rest thee, my babe, there's a spirit within thee.
A mystery thou art, though unblest and unshriven—
A thing of the earth, and a radiance of heaven;
A flower of the one, thou art fading and dying—
A spark of the other, thou'rt mounting and flying.

Farewell, my sweet baby, too early we sever,
I may come to thee, but to me thou shalt never:
Some angel of mercy shall lead and restore thee,
A pure living flame, to the mansions of glory.
The moralist's boast may sound prouder and prouder,
The hypocrite's prayer rise louder and louder;
But I'll trust my babe in her trial of danger,
To the mercy of Him that was laid in the manger.'

One might search the poets diligently and he would fail to find a more beautiful tribute to parental affection than that of the Bard's address to his youngest daughter. It is only possible to give a few words from it:

"And now, sweet child, one boon I crave—
And pout not, for that boon I'll have—
One kiss I ask for grandam's sake,
Who never saw thy tiny make;
And one for her who left us late,
Laid low, but not forgotten yet;
And thy sweet mother, too, the nearest
To thee and me, the kindest, dearest—
Thou sacred, blest memorial,
When I kiss thee, I kiss them all."

But our poet can vary his theme and his thought. "The Auld Man's Fareweel to His Wee House," "The Regret," "The Elegy," "A Father's Lament," "The Broken Heart," "An Aged Widow's Lament," "Maria Gray," "I Hae Naebody Now," "The Moon was A-Waning," "Farewell to Glen-Shalloch," "Maggy and Me," "Poor Little Jessie," "Good Night and Joy be wi' You A'," are among the most tender of lyrics in any or all countries. Take one stanza from Jessie's lament over her brother:

"I hae naebody now to look kind and caress me;
I look for a friend, but nae friend can I see;
I dinna ken what's to become o' poor Jessie,
The wirl has little mair pleasure for me.
It's lang sin' a lost baith my father and mother,
I'm simple, an' poor, an' forlorn on the way;
I had ane that I likit, an only dear brother,
My Willie—but he's lying cauld i' the clay."

22

We have all read Burns' "John Anderson, My Joe John," and love it for its worth as a perfect picture of two persons who had spent their lives together in complete trust. In "Maggy and Me" Hogg tells us of the pure affection that dwelt "in the cottage sae wee." Time forbids quoting more than a few lines:

"A' ye wha ne'er fand the straight road to be happy,
  Wha are nae content wi the lot that ye dree,
Come down to the dwellin' o' which I've been tellin',
  You'll learn it by looking at Maggy an' me."

Our poet was a noble type of the true loyalist. He was loyal to the lost cause of the Stuarts—a true Jacobite, and he was also loyal to his sovereign. The same one that gave us "Donald McDonald" that was sung throughout the country and stirred every heart to the core when the Corsican tyrant threatened to invade Britain, also gave us "Bonnie Prince Charlie," "Flora Macdonald's Farewell," and "McLean's Welcome." With Campbell's "Ye Mariners of England" we place Hogg's "Donald McDonald," and alongside of Burns' "Scots Wha Hae wi' Wallace Bled" we link "Cam' Ye by Athol, Lad wi' the Philabeg." From "McLean's Welcome" one stanza must suffice:—

"Come o'er the stream, Charlie,
  Dear Charlie, brave Charlie;
Come o'er the stream, Charlie,
  And dine with McLean
If aught will invite you,
Or more will delight you,
'Tis ready, a troop of our bold Highland men,
All ranged on the heather
With bonnet and feather,
Strong arms and broad claymores,
  Three hundred and ten."

To a lofty tune Burns sang:—

- "Lay the proud usurpers low!
  Tyrants fall in every foe!
  Liberty's in every blow.—
    Let us do or die!"

23

In a voice as clear we hear Hogg:—

"Down through the Lowlands, down wi' the Whigga-
more.
Loyal true Highlanders, down wi' them rarely!
Ronald and Donald, drive on wi' the broad claymore,
Over the necks of the foes of Prince Charlie!

The one was pouring out his heart on his country's altar, the other his devotion to the Stuart cause, and both gave us war songs that stand on a par with "On to the Battle," "The Star Spangled Banner," and the "Marse laise Hymn." We must hasten on, and yet we are compelled to linger long enough to give "The Skylark:"

"Bird of the wilderness,
    Blithesome and cumberless,
Sweet be thy matin o'er moorland and lea!
    Emblem of happiness,
    Blest is thy dwelling place,
Oh, to abide in the desert with thee.

Wild is thy lay and loud,
    Far in the downy cloud,
Love gives it energy, love gave it birth.
    Where, on thy dewy wing,
    Where art thou journeying?
Thy lay is in heaven, thy love is in earth.

O'er fell and fountain sheen,
    O'er moor and mountain green,
O'er the red streamer that heralds the day,
    Over the cloudlet dim,
    Over the rainbow's rim,
Musical cherub, soar, singing away!

Then when the gloaming comes,
    Low in the heather blooms
Sweet will thy welcome and bed of love be!
    Emblem of happiness,
    Blest is thy dwelling place—
Oh, to abide in the desert with thee!"

Third, Hogg's attitude to the supernatural. Our poet was a profound believer in a Supreme Being who did all things well. His simple creed could be told in the words: "Whatever is, is right." In all his crosses and sorrows and losses, he never once wavered in his faith, nor turned aside from the narrow path, or lost sight of the star that had guided the shepherds long centuries ago. For him God ever lives and loves. When the mother's heart is full of sorrow as she watches her dying baby, he makes her say:—

"Some angel of mercy shall lead and restore thee,
    A pure living flame, to the mansions of glory."

The father weeping over his lost daughter can look beyond the present into the future with perfect resignation:—

"I blame not Providence's sway,
    For I have many joys beside,
Yet, oh! the blank at my right hand
    Can never be made up to me!"

The maiden, whose heart is breaking because her lover has proven unfaithful, can speak of heaven as kind. She can tell her father in the midst of it all:—

"Oh, let me be, and weep my fill
    O'er wounds that heal can never;
And O, kind Heaven! were it thy will
    To close these eyes forever."

As a hymn of resignation few finer examples can be found anywhere than the one "To the Deity." From it we take these words:—

"Then here thy footstool of mercy I bow,
    Imploring thy grace to deliver;
For shadows of darkness beleaguer me now,
    And I fly to my God and forgiver,
        For ever! O ever!
    I'll cling to my Saviour for ever."

In Hogg's time the religious life of the people had gone down sadly in many places; but he dwelt much on the struggles of the Covenanters for freedom of conscience. He had recalled before his mind the many trials they had endured and dangers they had braved, and has given us some of his finest poems on these days of stress and storm. One of the most inspiring and victorious of death songs in any language is that of "The Covenanter on the Scaffold." It reveals the poet in one of his most powerful moods, showing how man can rise superior to all the evil forces of the tyrant:—

"Sing with me! Sing with me!
Weeping brethren, sing with me!
For now an open heaven I see,
And a crown of glory laid for me.
How my soul this earth despises!
How my heart and spirit rises!
Bounding from the flesh I sever;
World of sin, adieu forever!"

From these few and short selections an estimate may be made of the faith with which the Ettrick poet could "look from nature u to nature's God." We here think of the opening and closing stanzas of Tennyson's "In Memoriam" as being peculiarly descriptive of our poet's spiritual convictions:—

"Strong Son of God, Immortal Love,
Whom we, that have not seen Thy face,
By faith, and faith alone, embrace,
Believing where we cannot prove.

"That God, which ever lives and loves,
One God, one law, one element,
And one far-off divine event,
To which the whole creation moves."

Having said thus much, some may ask with a cynical smile, What is the value of these writings? What is the value of the story that tells us what our forefathers did? What is the use of a song that utters only a Jacobite sentiment? Those who speak in such terms know not what they say. A very wise son of Scotland, Fletcher of Saltoun, in his letter to the Marquis of Montrose, said, "If a man were permitted to make all the ballads, he need not care who should make the laws of a nation." The songs and the stories of a people tell us of the real life of that people. It was Handel who said that Scotland had the finest songs in the world. The English historian, Froude, has said, "If we except the Athenians and the Jews, no people so few in number have scored so deep a mark in the world's history as the Scots have done. No people have a juster right to be proud of their blood." In the accomplishment of this we must give the song a foremost place.

On this subject John Stewart Blackie, a worthy exponent of Scottish song and an eminent Greek and Latin scholar, declared: "I have a great respect for Latin and Greek, but if the choice were to be made between two alternatives—Classical education and Scottish song—I would say at once, burn Homer, burn Aristotle, fling Thucydides into the sea, but let us by all means on our Scottish hills and by our Scottish streams have 'Highland Mary,' 'Auld Lang Syne,' "Scots Wha Hae wi' Wallace Bled,' and 'When the Kye Comes Hame." Personally, I am not ashamed to say that I have through life got more healthy stimulus to the best part of my nature from half a dozen Scottish popular songs than from all the volumes that I ever spurred my way through of Roman or Hellenic minstrelsy." Such is the opinion of one of Scotland's sanest and greatest of scholars and critics. Towards the making of the songs of Scotland that he placed so high, James Hogg played a part only second ˙ that of the immortal Robert Burns.

Many have been the attempts to compare Hogg with Burns and Scott. This may be interesting, but it will not yield much fruit. A more profitable course would be that of contrasting these remarkable men. Burns was the poet of the human passions. He saw men and women as they were. He held in full view their frailties and their virtues. He knew their loves and their bitter hates. He worked at white heat, and his intense and consuming feeling was the moving spring of all his singing. He was as a volcano ever bursting forth and pouring its molten material in all directions. He could not control himself; for he was under the control of an impelling force within himself. He is a Sappho and a Horace combined.

Scott was like the broad and mighty river that swept on in the fulness of its tide through the great country of romance. In his prose and his poetry he brings us into living contact with the past. His writings glide on as if too massive to be disturbed by the unevennesses that may lie at the bottom of the stream. There is no violent outburst of passion; there is no irresistible display of emotion, there is no tornado; all is as the undulating plain, the lofty and solemn mountain, the onward flow of the river, and the broad ocean beyond. Whole armies are passed before the eye rather than the consuming fire in some human soul. He moves with the grandeur of a Homer or a Virgil. Scott speaks of forests, mountains, rivers, lakes, armies; Burns sees the wounded hare, the frightened mouse, the crushed daisy, the shivering cattle, the lovely maiden, the banks and braes, and he draws his world-wide and world-wise morals from them all.

· Hogg stands apart .from these, unique and alone. We might say of him thus:—

"A solitary rock in a far distant sea
   Rent by the thunder's shock an emblem
      stands of thee."

Hogg was ever on the hilltop looking, on the one hand, into the sun and beyond it, and, on the other, viewing the quiet scenery beneath, and what men were doing there, guided by the spirit world above. He was ever rising from the natural to the supernatural; turning his thoughts from the material to the spiritual world. Through the mists that overhang the river he sees the spirits of the departed, the subdued shades of the gloaming bring with them the witching hour. He takes his pilgrims far away into the cerulean depths beyond the circuit of the sun, and shows them the vast universe, and then brings them safely back again to sing to them that sweet pastoral "When the Kye Comes Hame." His "Skylark" is less of a bird than a spirit, for it pierces the blue dome above the rainbow's rim. "Little Pynkie" is a blend between a child of the earth and one of the sky, and when she wheels in her magic dance she holds her spectators spellbound, and makes them join in her fairy circlings. Kilmeny is spirited away, and brought back again a creature of indescribable beauty. The great poets of the imagination, Shelley and Shakespeare, claim him as one of their own.

Burns drew his poetic visions from a con-

suming fire that was ever burning within him;
Scott was inspired by the great volume of the
romance of the past; Hogg was impelled by
the spirit world, looking over the balconies of
heaven upon the events of this earth. We
now leave him among his great companions,
raised on a monument of his own most cunning
workmanship, and on that monument we
lovingly place the eulogy of Mark Antony
over the departed Brutus:—

> "His life was gentle, and the elements
> So mixed in him that nature could stand up
> And say to all the world, "this was a man.""

WS - #0009 - 190923 - C0 - 229/152/2 [4] - CB - 9780331703870 - Gloss Lamination